Will You Be My Flower Girl?

Activity and Sticker Book

Dear _____,

Will you be my Flower Girl?

Love, _____

Lulu Hart • illustrated by **Lesley Breen Withrow**

BLOOMSBURY
Activity Books

NEW YORK LONDON OXFORD NEW DELHI SYDNEY

YOU ARE INVITED!

JOIN US
FOR THE **WEDDING** OF

_____ &

_____

Date: _____

Time: _____

Location: _____

We can't wait to
celebrate with you!

Decorate the invitation with sticker hearts, flowers, and more.

Who would you invite to the wedding? Write a list or draw pictures of the family and friends you hope will be there!

THE WEDDING PARTY

A Flower Girl is part of the Wedding Party, a group of special friends and family that will stand with the couple on the wedding day. Sometimes it includes a Maid of Honor, Bridesmaids, a Best Man, Groomsmen, and of course a Flower Girl! Don't forget the Ring Bearer, too.

The Flower Girl's job is to spread flower petals down the aisle at the wedding.

The Ring Bearer brings the wedding rings. You throw the petals, but he better not toss those rings!

Look out for the rings on every page of this book! Don't let them get lost!

DRESS-UP TIME!

You will wear a beautiful dress at the wedding! How would you design it?

Color and decorate the dress.

Draw a new design, all your own!

Find stickers in the back to add flowers and bows!

What about the bride's dress?
Help her decide which gown
to wear!

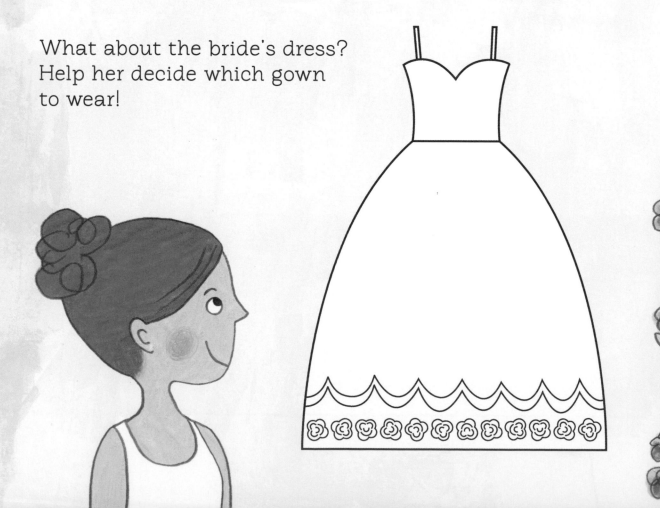

Can you match her earrings and necklaces? Which set is best for the big day?

FLOWERS FOR EVERYONE

Brides and bridesmaids carry beautiful bouquets!
Can you color the bride's bouquet?

You can ask the bride:
What are the wedding
colors? What flowers
would you pick?

Which bouquets match the bridesmaid dresses?

Flower girls carry a basket of flowers or petals to scatter down the aisle at the wedding. Decorate your basket!

Count the petals on each flower.
Which one will give you the most
petals to sprinkle on the aisle?

You'll practice doing your flower girl duties at the rehearsal. Walk nice and slowly down the aisle, and spread your petals on the ground to make a special path for the bride!

_____ Who goes next? Listen carefully at the rehearsal and then write numbers above the heads of the wedding party to put the procession in the right order.

Groom

Bridesmaid

Ring Bearer

Bride

Best Man

Groomsman

Maid of Honor

IT'S THE WEDDING DAY!

The guests are starting to arrive. Where will they sit?
Follow the lines to help the guests find their seats.

WHAT HAPPENS AT THE WEDDING?

The bride and groom make vows—their promises
to be partners and to love and care for each other.
Then they exchange rings.

Oh, no! The rings are missing!
Can you find them?

PHEW! THEY GOT MARRIED!

Next, we take pictures with the whole wedding party. Draw your wedding party. Draw the happy couple. Draw yourself in your beautiful dress!

PRESENTS!

Guests bring gifts for the newlyweds. Color the gift table,
then find the present stickers in the back and arrange
them here. Will they all fit?

NEXT, IT'S TIME FOR THE RECEPTION

Every table should be set the same—can you spot the differences? There are at least six!

Fill in the name cards. Who sits where?

YAY, CAKE!

How would you decorate the wedding cake? Color and add stickers to make a delicious-looking confection!

AT THE RECEPTION, IT'S TIME TO DANCE!

Seek and find: Where is the bride? The ring bearer? The cake, the bouquet, two bridesmaids, someone feeling shy? Someone very sleepy?

THIS HAS BEEN A VERY SPECIAL DAY!

Share your favorite memories of the wedding.

SONGS WE DANCED TO

_____

_____

_____

_____

_____

FOOD WE ATE

_____

_____

_____

_____

_____

WHAT A DAY!

What are the ring bearer and flower girl dreaming about?